THE WALL STREET JOURNAL.

Portfolio of

Golf Cartoons

THE WALL STREET JOURNAL.

Portfolio of

Golf Cartoons

Edited by CHARLES PRESTON

Published by

THE WALL STREET JOURNAL.

DOWJONES

ISBN 1-881944-33-6

Books can be purchased in bulk at special discounts.
For information please call (800) 635-8349, Dow Jones & Company.

The Wall Street Journal
200 Liberty Street
New York, NY 10280

Printed in the United States of America
1 2 3 4 5 6 7 8
First Edition

THE WALL STREET JOURNAL.

Portfolio of

Golf Cartoons

"This is my fifth 'Tiger' this month."

"I'll be back later, Dear.
I'm going out to build some humility."

"Look, a harbinger of spring."

"We have irreconcilable
differences—he thinks
golf is only a game."

"His qualifications are excellent—good references,
five years' practical experience and he
shoots in the low 80s."

"I'll *do the muttering around here!*"

*"About this loss of 38 golf balls in the water
and 47 in the woods last year—"*

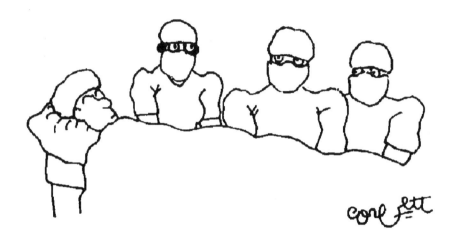

"*Five-iron. I mean, scalpel . . .*"

"How can I concentrate with that thump! thump! thump! of your heart beating!"

"*I believe the Scots invented this game,
and they also invented the bagpipe. Believe me,
they have a lot to answer for.*"

"I was really clobbering her until
she got lucky on the last seventeen holes."

"I'll bet you three referrals I can sink this putt."

"I understand this course
was designed by an attorney."

"*We must be getting close to civilization.*"

"So you want to play hardball, huh, Clayton?"

"*Mr. Caldwell declared victory and went to the golf course. May I take a message?*"

"Trouble is, you're letting a minor economic adjustment on Wall Street ruin your whole golf picture."

"Score! I don't want to know my score!
I play for relaxation. . . . See!"

*"He's the sharpest prosecutor I've
ever faced—but on the golf course
I destroy him!"*

"Before we were married you conceded all my putts up to 10 feet!"

"I'm told that on the golf course,
he's a mover and a shaker."

"Fred?"

*"OK guys, let's go, should the rain
increase we can always quit!"*

"*Got stuck in a sand trap with him once.*
He sold me $500,000 insurance before I got out."

"If you ask me, Bob, I don't think
iron man golf is going to catch on."

"Psst, want to beat Woods, Faldo, Kite. . . ?"

*"At my age it's harder getting the ball
out of the hole than getting it in . . ."*

"I'll concede your putt if you'll concede mine!"

"It's called 'Frustration.'"

"No, those aren't crickets you're hearing,
they're beepers."

"*Aft!*"

"*I hate the game, but it's the only pleasure I have.*"

"It's a Swiss army golf club."

"*Are you sure it's not out of your way?*"

"I recognize that glazed look, Harry.
You're reliving that hole-in-one,
aren't you?"

"Gosh, did he get the breaks—
71 shots in a row."

"If you get discouraged, this liquid-center
ball comes in bourbon, rye and scotch!"

"*I didn't think lying about fish or golf counted.*"

"The game bores me,
but I need the exercise."

*"Why don't you think of it as
sparing you the anguish of shooting
another 110?"*

"Oh, we're just crunching some numbers."

"So what are your plans for tomorrow. . . ?"

"*What I mean honey, is after* us,
my first priority is my golf game."

"Stop *fetching!*"

*"When the dating service said
you loved greens, I thought
they meant vegetables."*

"*Saint Andrew, I presume . . .*"

*"It breaks just a teensy bit to the right
. . . and did I mention hit it firm?"*

"The golfers are delivered unto us!"

"I shot a sixty-eight on the math test."

"It's snowing . . . that means
we'll have to start using
colored golf balls."

*"Maybe you should have worn
your Jack Nicklaus shirt."*

"It's the Bill Gates hole—a hard drive
and a soft chip gets you in the green."

"Is the club going through another financial crisis?"

DIVOTS

CALDWELL.

"I'm seriously thinking of replacing this artificial turf with real grass."

"*I've been retired a month
and already I hate this game.*"

"You should have known better than to kiss
your putter in this icy weather."

"*I know where I am—where the hell is my ball!*"

STEIN

"Delusions of grandeur, eh? What you need is to take up golf!"

*"I think you should spot me a few strokes.
After all, you're an M.B.A."*

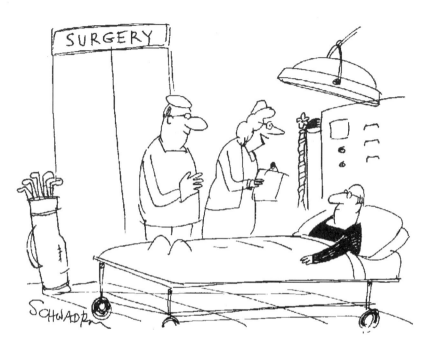

"Don't worry, there isn't a steadier hand than Dr. Henpenny who shoots in the low 70s."

"*You have to avoid excitement at all costs—go home and watch some golf on television.*"

"*Wake up, Leroy! You're sleep-putting again.*"

"Furgis, when I said 'See you on the links,'
I meant Web page links."

"I'll look for the ball. You look for the club."

Index of Cartoonists

Charles Preston edits the "Pepper . . . and Salt" cartoon feature, which appears daily on the editorial pages of The Wall Street Journal and WSJ.com. To subscribe, call 1-800-JOURNAL or go to http://services.wsj.com.